Sarah Salway

Learning Springsteen on my language app

Indigo Dreams Publishing

First Edition: Learning Springsteen on my language app
First published in Great Britain in 2023 by:
Indigo Dreams Publishing
24, Forest Houses
Cookworthy Moor
Halwill
Beaworthy
Devon
EX21 5UU
www.indigodreamspublishing.com

Sarah Salway has asserted her right under the Copyright, Designs and Patents Act 1988 to be identified as the author of this work.

ISBN 978-1-912876-76-1

British Library Cataloguing in Publication Data. A CIP record for this book can be obtained from the British Library.

Designed and typeset in Palatino Linotype by Indigo Dreams.
Cover design by Ronnie Goodyer at Indigo Dreams
Printed and bound in Great Britain by 4edge Ltd.

Papers used by Indigo Dreams are recyclable products made from wood grown in sustainable forests following the guidance of the Forest Stewardship Council.

For Bri and Mags

Acknowledgements

Thank you to the editors of the following publications and competitions where some of these poems first appeared, at times in earlier versions: The Phare, Agenda Magazine, Finished Creatures, Obsessed with Pipework, Brittle Star, Manchester Cathedral Poetry Competition, The Rialto, Frogmore Press, Poetry Wales, Ink Sweat and Tears, South Magazine, and the Kent & Sussex Poetry Society Folio.

Thank you to the editors of Indigo Dreams for all you do. I'm very proud to be one of the Geoff Stevens Memorial Prize winners.

I'm grateful for the chance to work with the artist, Perienne Christian, via the Alde Valley Festival residencies on several of these poems.

Some of the poems from The Year in Short were taken from my chapbook, *Let's Dance,* published by Coast to Coast to Coast as an artist's edition created by Maria Isakova Bennett.

The poem 'Sitting in on the Adult Literacy Class' was inspired by a visit to Ruskin's Readers in London. It was a reminder of the power of reading, and how much we can take it for granted. I'm grateful for all readers.

CONTENTS

Learning Springsteen on my language app

A Dictionary of How to Live Properly

It's always out on loan but I know it must exist
because I can spot everyone who's read it,

and then the others, like me, who still hope
to rise to the top of the waiting list. Sometimes

when I'm in the library, I'll pause by the gap
in the shelf where it should be sitting.

Once I even licked the covers of the two books
on either side. I ignore the tuts of the librarian,

pretend not to see how she fusses over that plant
on her desk. I hate that orchid, its white roots

the legs of a hospital patient trying to escape,
and the time she spends on it would be better

used helping some of us find the one book
we need. *Orchids stand for death,* I told her once,

but she smiled, told me it had bloomed
three times already. *Just needs proper care,*

she says. The speckles round her mouth dance
as she tells me the Dictionary doesn't exist

and besides she doesn't like
the way I stand so close to her desk,

while other readers bustle by,
getting on – properly – with their lives.

Sitting in on the Adult Literacy Class

DRY
After a life on shifting seas, his son
asks, *why bother?* But he's pinning
himself down to this new world,
word by word by word.

FLY
Listen to these scribbles on the page,
read the pictures with me,
here are the days:
Tuesday, Wednesday, Sunday.

WHY
Yes, in some circumstances,
a y does sounds like an i,
put two consonants together,
feel your tongue move forward.

SLY
The words move too quickly,
out of reach, just like our days,
and see, day is a different kind of Y.

CRY
I agree it doesn't always make sense.
Let's try again.

Folded

The child's tongue bleached into silence
     after too many
               hot
words, and it is her mother
        who folds the sound
  back into her like
        taming
            sheets
freshly
      freed
             from the washing line
a corner of daughter in each hand
holding sure to the edges
as the girl walks towards
and back,
towards and back,
a mess of material the mother catches,
holds tight next to her heart before
stepping
          away for the next stretch,
moving
    a little closer each time
until they both declare it done,
the smoothest bundle they've ever seen,
the sweetest song.

Survival

We didn't know where the cloud came from
or when it first appeared on our street,
it was just there one day, blocking out the sun
so we had to check our clocks.
Was it really morning?
Some of us stayed in bed
while others carried on business as usual.
We were kind at first
but soon it was easier to imagine
the old couple at number seven
were on holiday, blinds still down,
and really wasn't it better for mothers
to care for their own families,
who wants do-gooders in dark times?
We were proper citizens though when the man
on the corner filled his house with the homeless,
at least then the police came quickly.
We got used to looking down,
pretending our shoulders weren't stressed
with carrying this new burden,
and maybe all would have been well –
survival of the fittest graffitied
on every church wall – if one of us
hadn't started to leave flowers
on doorsteps, a simple daisy,
white rose, sprig of rosemary,
and the apple trees hadn't blossomed
twice as if beauty still mattered
and there would be enough to scatter
even where it might never be found.

Does a ton of feathers weigh the same as a ton of bricks?

Words drop like feathers,
I've never told anyone this before....
our trails of conversation
are white clouds floating behind us.
We still take secret phone calls
we can't bring back to the party
but these new syllables are so heavy,
medication... safe... sorry...
When you're listening so hard
and being heard back,
it makes you vulnerable,
when *I've been thinking...*
weighs as much as *Is that an egret?*
it makes you stronger than you've ever been.
I care for you so much...
we've flown to the sun,
all of us who tend this fire,
Do you remember...
we know how precious it is
to land safely back on earth.

Ignition

Late again for yoga, I run past the sudden flame of red leaves
as they reach out over a suburban wall. The heat of it still
burns as I stretch into Downward Dog, smoulders through
Tree and blazes in Warrior Two. Even a cautious Dolphin
can't put it out. I try to breathe in the cool air from the open
studio windows, to concentrate on where I am, to focus my
intentions on peace, but all I can think about is that radio
interview, a woman saying how she always tells at least
one friend where she is, when she is leaving, where she
is going, in case they need to find her body. All those moments
when I too was just walking home.

red dots on phone maps
chorus of urgent whispers
graves may lie here

Echo in the workshop

By the end of the poem
the poet must be changed,
otherwise it's just narcissism

As we work to her set tasks
the teacher reapplies scarlet lipstick,
licks her teeth as if she tastes blood.

We all have obsessions
even if you think your subject is ducks
you'll find you're writing about ---

I have written a poem about ducks,
I make a note to dig it out,
see what's swimming underneath.

She's flicking through her notes now,
looks at the clock then round the room
as if disappointed we're all still there

Introduce windows into your poem,
cut the start and end if necessary,
ask yourself where is the surprise.

My new home has lots of windows,
I'm obsessed with the colour of wood.
Carefully I look back at my draft

while across the room, someone sobs
because her poem is changing her life.
Buy lipstick, I write in the margin.

Learning Springsteen on my language app

I had high hopes after my friend Sian fell in lust
with a tattooed teacher-bot, but she's a red headed
woman and I'm just so many spare parts,

shackled and drawn with no promised land.
I ain't got you because how can they save
love when even my much practised

'Does this bus stop at 82nd street' is met
with 'Dream baby dream'. Word by word,
I've been dancing in the dark, proving

it all night but still the app wants more:
no surrender, no reason to believe. It's living
proof there's a radio nowhere, not even one step

up from my year of speaking Justin Beiber.
Wait for me, cautious man, because if
this is the real world, I wanna marry you.

You're my reason to believe the world can
understand each other. Silence is the price
you pay when there's no human touch,

so knock down the wall, the ties that bind,
I'm on fire, this is a New York City serenade
and I'm out on the street, my sentences

are winning roulette chips, each verb a stolen car
driving straight into the fire, and see that noun,
there goes my miracle.

'She did her best'

It split us all, that epitaph
on a mid-West grave
as friends I thought I knew
wished for something similar.
Didn't they see, as I did, a list
of impossible chores, no time to dream
or eat ripe peaches peeled by a man
with his own pocketknife?

It's important to discuss how we want
to be remembered –
so many here falling asleep,
or merely resting. And it seems
we are defined by relatives
long after they too are forgotten,
wife of – aunt of – sister of –
devoted more times than beloved.

I'm not sure *She did her best*
will ever be said of me,
Maybe *She wanted the best*,
and, ah, there it is,
finding always in the act of writing
the truth: a simple gravestone,
to die with all my words used up but one –

more.

words

why do some words
taste of salt and honey?
–

letters tapdancing
over the page,
soft-shoe percussion
–

an armchair
an open book
time holds its breath
–

little bookworm
eating her way
into the world
–

turning the page
during an African summer –
snow out the window
–

past bedtime
and the page
hugs tighter
–

sleepless at night
bookshelves arrange
in rows of possible selves
–

the reader in the book
the book in the tree
the tree in the earth

In the queue outside the Museum of Light

We glitter with excitement,
snake past our shadows.
We are all ages, all shapes,
carrying our common aim
like a candle to bed.

Words from the loudspeaker
tinsel around us,
and when the doors open
we are full-hearted.
More than one of us slept
clutching their ticket last night.

A neon *'Love Me'* in lipstick pink
nestles by an early morning shock
of hunter's lights through pines.

It's a relief to pause before streetlights
on a rainy afternoon in Aberystwyth,
a string of circus lights,
candelabras lit once a year.

Is this how they do it? Draw us in
like magnets to the corners
we still hope might shine for us,
gentled by the touch of a child's
nightlight sending rainbow animals
to dance on the walls

until without warning, they flick off
the switches, and we're sent back
into the darkness, feeling
our way to the end of the tunnel .

Why it's no fun being me at night

Each creak on the wooden staircase
in our holiday flat
is a man, always a man,
with a curved knife as long as himself,
creeping to where I mock-sleep
so he'll move on,
take only our money, passports,
and of all the things
I hope the killer doesn't take,
why is it the olive oil the chef
gave us last night?
How he pressed it
into my hands saying, *not for frying*,
as if he knows I'm a woman who eats fried food,
and now I see the bottle breaking in our suitcase
on the flight home, so many clothes
ruined. How much money
have I spent when there are so many children
hungry for bread in the world,
when I ate almost the whole basket
at supper dipping it in olive oil
like a woman who doesn't know when to say no,
but all those times I said no when I should have said yes.
Just yesterday I could have had a last swim
with my husband, my husband
who is snoring now as if he doesn't know
he's just been murdered. I should have leapt
in the sea with him while I could,
instead of sitting on rocks
pretending to watch while all the time

I was writing a poem about death,
and even now, instead of jumping up
and rescuing us both,
I'm worrying over that last line:
is it the body or the life that's temporary,
and why was that any kind of comfort
anyway, and should we get
some bubblewrap for the olive oil?

I want to be like all the women

on my Pinterest moodboard
but I've never worn a white shirt
all day and kept it clean.
In fact I spend most of my time
in yoga kit, hoping the postman
will think I can spring
from free-weights to handstand
like that photograph
of a boss woman who juggles
two screens while feeding her baby,
and though it's true, the postman
hardly calls these days,
and I don't need to be dressed
to answer emails, a business shirt
casually waist-tied gives
a certain flourish like the kiss
I sometimes add, delete, add
to my signature. I like
how these women
gaze through the screen,
looking not just into the sun
that always shines on them,
but as if they can see me,
standing in front of a bubbling pot
of tomato sauce, a sisterhood
of pristine white shirts willing
me on, none of us spilling a drop.

My son made friends with a bubble
(Edinburgh Science Festival 1998)

Maybe this is how it'll be
when we finally meet again,
the afternoon I briefly looked away
only to find him up on stage, my shy boy,
his face frozen as he realised everyone
was staring and there was nothing
to do but stay as the scientist told him
– pop – to touch the – pop – bubbles
streaming from the – pop – sidelines
but not to – pop – keep breaking – pop – them,
and only when I thought I couldn't bear it,
would have to run up and stop this game,
his hands were plunged into soapy water
until his bubbles met their bubbles
so when he caught one between his fingers
it stayed whole on his skin, glistening
like that new expression on his face.
Look, the scientist said, *they are friends now*
and how loudly we all clapped
so when he walked back to me,
he still shone with pride.
Yes that's how we'll be, gently covered
in our best selves, making new memories
as – pop – we say – pop – I've missed you.

Skull

It stares back at us
through an iron grille,
its wooden casket a jumble
of bones we try to identify –
hip, knee, ankle – a parody
of the children's song
that makes us giggle.

The skull doesn't change
its expression, we swear
it's disappointed with how
its life has come to this while
across the aisle, the labelled body
of an embalmed saint
is surrounded by flowers, candles
and tourists paying respect.

But you (because you've become
our skull now) have caught us
by surprise so you come with us
as we walk out into Pisa, carried
shoulder high in our stories
about who you were, how you
ended up there and the question
most often asked of saints:
what could you do for us?

Over lunch of anchovy crostini
in a backstreet café, I tell the story
of one saint's bones sent
across the world, *Veloce* written
on the box's side. St Quick
is still prayed to for release,
legal transactions, the ability
to meet an impossible deadline.

We sip red wine, eat pasta
cooked *al dente,* a gelato
so good we can't speak, and when
the blue haired chef comes out
to shake our hands, we see the pattern
of multi-coloured skulls on her apron:
patron saints of slow hidden pleasures,
coming across beauty unprepared.

In fields of dandelion clocks

As I write this, a caterpillar lands
on my still blank page,
I wonder what ice cream
made from bluebells would taste like
and why hawthorn turns wool pink,

from the books I've time to read
I learn that the word 'landscape'
really comes from land craftsmanship
and that Capability Brown invented
the phrase *to move mountains.*

Every day outside my window
the world's longest picnic table
is taking shape and from my cowslip garden
I hear strangers share secrets
and lost wishes.

When it all gets too much,
I head for the woods
so that later when my husband rings
to ask if I've heard the news
I tell him that a swarm of bees
has landed on an apple tree
and I've heard six different bird songs.

Not that news, he starts. *At least six,* I say,
because time moves differently
in fields of dandelion clocks,
a tuning fork vibrating
as the butterfly unfurls.

My father takes Rupert Brooke's poems to France, 1945

You'll have to believe me when I say
each disc from this stem of honesty
is thicker than the pages
of the book of poems my father
took to war with him. I like to think
it was the weight behind each word
that kept him pushing to a future
he couldn't dare write himself:
to love and be so loved.
Though once reading fairy tales
to us at bedtime, he leant so far
into that night's story
I started crying, sensing how
he wanted to topple into it,
just as he must have done –
above the stench of mud and blood –
to smell Brooke's sweet honey and tea.

Loving Trees

A hospital at Halloween - the joke is lost
as we wait in a white room, talk about weather,
stare at passing doctors, each face a mask
of unchipped stone. The empty corridor smells
of death, dusty with autumn leaves
flaked in mud. You tell me you love trees.

It's been a good year for trees,
but maybe less for people. We are lost
and heavy, carrying sadness like bad weather.
It's not the fabric masks we wear, but the mask
of pretending how we're coping that smells
of what it's been like, how we want to leave

it all behind now, like the pang I feel as you leave
to get us coffee. From the window I see trees,
perhaps there's a forest where we could get lost,
make a new home, a nest safe in all weathers,
covered in mushroom and bark, our mask
stripped off, communicate by touch and smells,

but you rush back – the coffee smells
like morning – because you've seen the surgeon leave.
Suddenly we're wind-wobbling like trees,
is this a good sign or is all lost?
This room suddenly opens to the weather,
Can you be sure, I cry, *without his mask?*

The nurse has soft-soled shoes, a blue mask
that can't hide her disgust at the animal smell
of our panic. She says it'll be fine, we should leave,
go home, have a bath, sleep. That night the trees
round the car park muffle our conversation. *We'll be lost,*
we sweep, *without her.* It's winter weather

as we hug, strange what I remember – the weather
and not how I felt when the phone call came. We mask
our own sadness to protect others. The funeral smells
of candles and lilies. *It's a good way for her to leave,*
we murmur, *surrounded by love and buried near trees.*
Sometimes the only way to win is to be lost.

Years later, lost and alone, I write her a card: *weather
is here, wish you were awful.* Jokes are masks that smell
of what we wish we hadn't left. Do you still love trees?

Perhaps all adult orphans are unarmoured

The story rolls itself out like linen knots
caught under worn pattern pieces,

scissors nosing their way round darts
and pleats, and although the first cut

is hard, soon every dart of the needle
weakens the threads to my past.

No longer will I put my hands
in pockets of an old coat

to pull out my father's glasses,
or find a shopping list my mother wrote.

It's time to restitch my self.

No use crying

over the stitch you didn't save,
the step you forgot to take.

It's been years since she died –
popped her clogs, kicked the bucket –
and yet here she is, flitting across

my eye line to whisper in my ear –
that black cat, good or bad? – until
it's as if there's a little goblin inside –

leave a bit out for the fairies –
because my body remembers her,
her mother and all the mothers before,

so when I salute the single magpie –
morning jack, morning jack, morning jack –
and look across to see my children

raise their hands too – *blood's thicker*
than – I know it's these small pebbles
of half-forgotten meaning that shape

our landscape, provide shelter
when we need it, pave the roads
on which we travel to reach home.

Nothing needs to make perfect sense,
just to pop out unexpectedly like a song
we've always known the rhythm to,

better safe than sorry, better late than never,
don't count your chickens, who's she –
the cat's mother? Time to mop up the milk.

Cryptic

I've never eaten a kebab
on the way home from a night clubbing
or worn another woman's pants,
water-skied in a bikini or climbed a tree
higher than my house.

I don't know why it's wrong to laugh in church
or why I had to study chemistry,
I don't like rough games or long bookless days.
I can't do a handstand, the splits
or a cryptic crossword. And many of these things
I can't do, I don't see the point of

but I have developed a fine ability
to sit quietly in hospital waiting rooms,
to hold your hand, to be the one you call
at four in the morning when you've nothing to say
and nobody to say it to.

And one day when it's all over,
I'll do a crossword, climb a tree.
I'll even try to laugh in church for you.

Shell Petrol Station, Bedford

I never stopped loving it,
still bend to press fingertips
in spilt petrol so, later, I can surprise
myself with a tilt of the stomach
simply by bringing my hand
to my face as if I don't know
what I'm doing, just as years ago,
my mother hadn't expected the car mechanic
to bend right through the window,
oblivious to me in the back,
to lay oil rimmed fingers on her shoulder.
How her stomach must have lurched
then too, wondering what might come next,
but the man righted himself
and we drove off, half laughing.
Only I, looking back, had seen him
raise a hand to his face as if he'd caught
the perfume my mother never wore again.

The Finishing Touch

Sometimes you think you'd like
to live in a perfectly white house,
white walls, white floors,

no pencil marks to mark how
the kids grew up too fast,
dog hairs impossible to brush off,

red wine stains from *that* party,
and pictures so familiar that if they flew off
walls, you could paint them back yourself.

There's silence in your white house,
it smells of … nothing. No messy meals
shared there, no familiar cushions to stroke,

it'd be like floating on a cloud,
like all those times you've looked down
from a plane, longing to jump out,

to let the air hold you until
you were ready to step back into life.

Driving past things I might have missed

We'd barely sat down to eat when, not
knowing what to talk about, a long story
involving cars pops out and then won't stop.
I tell the man beside me about the time
my parents gave a lift to a woman
who wore a fur coat and called her handbag
her *pocket book*. I tell him how I'd wanted
to feel that fur so badly I had to sit on my hands.

Around us, people are swapping small talk
about house prices, schools and holidays;
none of us know each other
apart from through work, but the way
we're not in office clothes tonight
makes us feel half-dressed, our hands
stay by our sides in case we should touch
another's skin, so his confession

of how he'd cried when a beloved aunt
on a rare visit walked out of church
to mistakenly get into a strangers' car,
and, that's not all, spent the weekend
with them, makes me wonder if it's not just cars
that feel like home, what makes some places

seem so safe? *I wish you'd stroked that coat,*
he says as the pudding arrives
and we turn away from each other,
begin to discuss the weather.

Stone Star
Altes Museum, Berlin

These blocks of stone
chipped from a Nubian temple,
have been numbered, crated,

We take care of all gods

until in the museum she becomes
a jigsaw to put together:
shoulders, toes, hands,

with our information boards,

we read her in the gaps:
her warrior face, that centre
stone a fisted feathered hand,

white gloves, controlled climate,

tunic of wings soaring
over hot red sand
inside the smooth clean frame –

visitors kept at a careful distance.

a pyramid
balanced
on one small bare foot.

Desire Path

I'm fearful of fever, floods,
and taking it on the chin,

so when you tell me to chant
to raise the world's vibration,

to be honest, I'm doubtful,
though luckily a daffodil

doesn't pause before singing
its spring song, bursting over

long forgotten paths. Flowers
are holding our old maps safe

as I bend forward to breathe
into each yellow trumpet,

wait as the earth settles, soothes.

Fixtures and Fittings

It started with the oven growing in the night
as we slept oblivious to the creaks and groans
of metal expanding against our kitchen walls,

and in the morning we moved out to the garden,
breakfast coffees perched on our knees
as we watched the fridge respond, teetering

back and forth, bulging into any space it found.
All that week, we kept busy buying more food,
lettuces regimented in lines, sausages for armies,

for it was war, and we were the foot soldiers
unsure of whose side we were on, except
it wasn't ours. Even sofas swelled, cushions smothered,

but they were incidental to the electricals,
television blasting headlines and secret kisses,
while the radio bored on and on. We gave up

wondering what was blending in the food processor
when red liquid splattered over floors and the Hoover
sucked it clean. The eternal whispering of the kettle

would have kept us awake if our beds had let us
sleep, duvets rapunzelling out of windows, and still
the oven and the fridge carried on their terrible dance,

gleaming metal against metal, souvenir magnets
of theme parks clashing with haiku fragments
and handwritten notes. So long as we carried on

shopping we felt safe, our arms lengthening
with the weight of all those bags, until it stopped,
suddenly, one day, a truce made somewhere,

the house shrank back to size, only the door
sticking in its frame as if it was warning us
how danger could be found inside as well as out.

Circular walk

You can't stop thinking
about the bench
in the nature reserve,
'We are just one breath.'

The bench is reserved
and you can't stop
breathing in nature.
Think, we are just one.

Stop, nature's benching,
can't think,
reserve breath.
We are just.

Think of the reserve
as just a bench.
Stop nature, can't you?
We are.

Bench stop,
just reserve
nature think.
You, we.

Reading a book on lost gardens

Endlessly sunny, with trees a line of dots
like small boys' knees in an old school photo

so I read it in the same way, a fascination
in the butterfly-pinned moment.

I stroke black and white grass, pick fruit
with my finger and thumb from walled gardens,

trace the serpentine walks I'd take, my full skirt
brushing at the knots until the scent of box

releases, each path could be a wish or a regret.
Can photographs be capable of happiness?

Because as I turn the page I see an open gate
beckoning to the future, and I bend with jealousy

at how they'll never watch each other grow old
or laugh at all that time left for flourishing.

The Lepidopterist

So many ways into the ancient stories, words hum in the air ...
try to catch some. You're a butterfly hunter, net alert for
meaning ... *congregation, sphere, trimmings* ... a birth next to a
death next to a marriage. Ah, you've got one, but before you
find a pin, it's flown away, a scrap torn in one corner, glue
unsticking. Against the hawthorn tree, a flat stone lies covered
in a layer of moss and a lone woman smiles under the headline,
Deep Sorrow. Turn the page.

The garden is the soft scaffolding to the heart

1.
A distant phone rings but you don't answer because it's your
dead mother who wants to complain of being lonely. She wants
to share what it's like there, but you need to stay with the
living, your bare feet on the wet grass. It hasn't always been
this way.

2.
The last owner of this house took abundant care over her plants
so they grew too big for such a small place. You talk to her all
the time you're in the garden, tell her how your mother had
said a tree would grow inside you when you once ate an apple
whole, core and all. You were excited, you say, kept rubbing
your hand over your hair to feel the nub of future branches.
You couldn't sleep that night because you were busy turning
into an orchard.

3.
Once a man you thought you might marry told you how every
time he played the cello, he would imagine he was making love
to the tree it came from. You try to listen to music as you dig up
the last owner's flower beds but all you can hear is spitting.

4.
There's a phone box in an American forest where you queue to
speak to your ancestors. You'd like to go there, if only to tell
your dead mother to stop ringing. Come spring, the bulbs
you've planted will have taken over the garden. You'll walk
around it, laugh at how you've assuaged the ghosts.

seeing light

at first light
before the sun's treasury
burns our path to gold
we lick our fingers
feel how the teasing sky
will play games
with the rest of our day

the inky secrets
of our dreams leak
away with every sip
of tea, fiery love
and salty sorrows
tempered with a dash
of milk

open the window
we can do this

the year in short

SPRING

and here it is again,
April rain
smelling
like three-day-old fish

deadheading too late,
my plants are old ladies
scattering stories
into the wind

in the candyfloss sky,
flying whales form a chariot
to race an indifferent sea

SUMMER

stone circles
and barefoot beaches,
island treasure

August bank holiday
on an English beach,
swim postponed

a tearoom secret
iced with lemon,
such sweet breath

pigeon blue sea
goosebumped skin,
not all birds migrate

AUTUMN

today is a robe
sliding from the world's shoulders
to safeguard the night

escaping from the street
to buy new books,
squirrels storing nuts
for cold days to come

November mist,
a pause before the world
clears back into itself

the holly's berries
are warning lights
as old wives whisper,
cold days ahead

WINTER

wind at the window,
we edge closer
listen to the trees

London evening
and the Christmas lights
are empty nests of diamonds

down a Piccadilly arcade
the smell of ripe cheese,
cigars and champagne,
money takes a shortcut

first frost,
spring comes calling
in a white box of bulbs

Rambling

This morning I'm in a trudge
of boots mindfully walking

to the river where I don't have
to swim, but will

because no-one makes me.
Here's the thing about mindfulness:

it makes you take responsibility
for yourself, and sometimes I just want

to be moss splattered like birdshit
on stone, or stuck in a cobweb

of dying branches unable
to read the *Danger of Death* sign.

Even those blackberries sweetening
and canoes piled up like toddler's crayons

are things I choose to notice.
How much more do I miss?

My mind's a man in green corduroy
telling me I've parked my car wrong.

Sod that. Today I am mindful
of how what goes by me is grass

growing hand-high, patiently waiting
to be ruffled. And lord, I'm ready for ruffling.

The Fine Art of Ravishing

I picture myself Victorian,
skirts frilled out on the ground,
forced to keep straight by a corset
a maid has tied too tight, gloves
slipping on the trowel, soiled satin
shoes, the lace on my hat
unbalancing me like a moth
caught in my hair, its veil covering
my eyes as I plant these poems
under sweetly scented rose bushes,

hoping they'll grow until a future woman,
untuned in the art of ravishing,
bends to pick these word flowers,
a polite vibration flowing down stems
until she hears voices bruised
by years of deadheading, thorns
prick her skin so each buried syllable,
every story that needs to be told
bubbles up like the blood
she licks clean with her tongue.

Tomorrow is the end of the world

It took some adjusting
but we're looking forward to it now.
Next Door have hung their bunting out,
lines and lines of LOVE and PEACE
which would have cost the earth
except there's no point in money now.
Shops had put up signs:
Take what you want.
Which was challenging.
What did we want?
Some families gathered together,
others stayed apart. By lunchtime,
most wished they'd picked the other option.
You and I, we kept to ourselves
although we sent *Good Luck* texts
to everyone in our contacts.
Drink was a balm. And sugar.
Netflix took our minds off things
until dusk when the electricity crashed.
What did we want?
Hot sex with strangers,
but even long-standing partners like us
could take on new shapes
when we knew this was the last time.
After a while though we got tired.
We blew dust off paper maps,
spread the world over our floor,
took turns in pointing,
That's where we'll go. Right there.
Our neighbours went to bed
but we watched their bunting
twist in the rising wind.
The Devil's coming, you said.
We hung up a mirror ball, danced.

Indigo Dreams Publishing Ltd
24, Forest Houses
Cookworthy Moor
Halwill
Beaworthy
Devon
EX21 5UU
www.indigodreamspublishing.com